To the reader:

Welcome to the DK ELT Graded Readers! These readers are different. They explore aspects of the world around us: its history, geography, science … and a lot of other things. And they show the different ways in which people live now, and lived in the past.

These DK ELT Graded Readers give you material for reading for information, and reading for pleasure. You are using your English to do something real. The illustrations will help you understand the text, and also help bring the Reader to life. There is a glossary to help you understand the special words for this topic. Listen to the cassette or CD as well, and you can really enter the world of the Olympic Games, the *Titanic*, or the Trojan War … and a lot more. Choose the topics that interest you, improve your English, and learn something … all at the same time.
Enjoy the series!

To the teacher:

This series provides varied reading practice at five levels of language difficulty, from elementary to FCE level:
BEGINNER
ELEMENTARY A
ELEMENTARY B
INTERMEDIATE
UPPER INTERMEDIATE
The language syllabus has been designed to suit the factual nature of the series, and includes a wider vocabulary range than is usual with ELT readers: language linked with the specific theme of each book is included and defined. The language scheme, and ideas for exploiting the material (including the recorded material) both in and out of class are contained in the Teacher's Resource Book. We hope you and your students enjoy using this series.

A DORLING KINDERSLEY BOOK

DK www.dk.com

Originally published as Eyewitness Reader
Movie Magic in 1999, text © 1999 Anne
Cottringer, and adapted as an ELT Graded Reader
for Dorling Kindersley by

studio cactus C

13 SOUTHGATE STREET WINCHESTER HAMPSHIRE SO23 9DZ

Published in Great Britain by
Dorling Kindersley Limited
9 Henrietta Street, London WC2E 8PS

2 4 6 8 10 9 7 5 3 1

A CIP catalogue record for this book is
available from the British Library.

ISBN 0-7513-3197-X

Colour reproduction by Colourscan, Singapore
Printed and bound in China by L. Rex Printing Co., Ltd
Text film output by Ocean Colour, UK

The publisher would like to thank the following
for their kind permission to reproduce their photographs:
Key: t=top, a=above, b=below, l=left, r=right, c=centre

Andrew Burgess: 12, 44–5; Dorling Kindersley Picture Library:
6, 7br, 10tr, 10tc, 13t, 26t, 28–9t, 42–3b, 43tr, 45br/ Dave King: 2, 23tr
/Evolution FX/Geoff Brightling: 34, 35tr, tc /Museum of the Moving
Image: 24t /Gary Ombler: 21cr, 21br, 22b; Garden Picture Library: 16b;
Kobal Collection: 9br, 20tr; National Motor Museum: 31tr;
Planet Earth Pictures: 39t; Polygram: "The Borrowers" 38;
Stock Market/Richard Borenholtz: 33b

Special thanks to Angels & Bermans Fancy Dress Shop
for permission to photograph the costumes on page 12
and Tony Child Post Production for permission
to photograph his editing equipment.

Contents

ELT Graded Readers

ELEMENTARY B

MOVIE MAGIC

Written by
George Woolard

Series Editor Susan Holden

London • New York • Delhi • Sydney

The Audition

Jo was standing on the stage of the school hall. A group of her friends and some adults were listening to her. Jo pointed upwards and shouted, "Oh, please let me come with you." Jo was talking to a spaceship, but it wasn't a real spaceship. She was only imagining that a spaceship was in the room.

Jo wanted to act in a film called *Starsearcher*. It was a science-fiction film about creatures from another planet. She was hoping to get a small part. This was her audition. Jo was excited but also a little nervous. "Pretend that the people are not there," she said to herself.

One of the adults in front of her was the film's casting director. It was the casting director's job to choose people to act in the film. She was a very important person and Jo was trying hard to impress her.

The director was at Jo's school because she wanted to find some young people for the film. She brought the film script and some storyboards with her.

The script of a film is a kind of book. It describes what happens in the film, and it contains all the words that the actors say. A storyboard is like a comic book. It explains the story in pictures.

Jo read the film script very quickly. The story happens on another planet somewhere in outer space. The planet is dying and some of the people try to save it.

Zara is the main character in the film and Zanuck is her younger sister. Zanuck wants very much to help her big sister. She thinks she can help her to save the planet.

This is a storyboard. The pictures show what happens in a film.

"Zanuck is the perfect part for me," thought Jo. "She's about the same age as me. I'll audition for that part."

Jo studied drama at school. When she read the lines of the script on stage, she tried to speak very clearly. She also tried to put some feeling into every word. When she was angry, she sounded angry. When she was happy, she looked and sounded happy.

5

Jo finished reading her part of the script. "I hope I've done well," she thought. "I really want to act in this film."

The film script may be changed many times.

The casting director got up from her seat. She had a camera in her hand and she took Jo's picture. "That's a good sign," thought Jo. Then the director did something Jo did not expect.

"Come down here, Jo," the director said. "I want to see how tall you are." The director took out a tape and measured Jo's height. She wrote it down in a small book. Jo was pleased. "I think she likes me," she thought.

Jo wanted to be Zanuck for another reason. Her favourite actor, Deborah Ray, was Zara in the film. "I have always wanted to meet her," Jo thought. "Now it might be possible."

As the director left the school, she said to the students, "We will telephone each of you in the next few days and tell you if you have been successful. Please be patient."

For three days, Jo could only think about the audition. She was very tense and restless. She couldn't read anything and she didn't sleep very well. "Why doesn't she phone me?"

Then one morning, her mother shouted, "Jo! There's a telephone call for you." Jo ran down the stairs from her bedroom and grabbed the phone from her mother. "Yes?" she said. Her hands were shaking. She was so excited.

Then she smiled and jumped up and down. She put the phone down and threw her arms around her mother. "I got the part, Mum. I got the part."

The next week, Jo and her parents went to the film studio.
A long black car took them there. Jo felt like a film star.

They met a lawyer from the film company and Jo's parents
signed a contract for her. They also signed a special form to
say that they were happy for Jo to be in the film.

In the studio, Jo felt very excited. "Just think,"
she thought, "Deborah Ray and me in the same film!"

A contract to act
Film actors sign contracts with the film
studio before the filming begins. The
contract usually describes the actor's job and
how much money the actor gets. If the actor
is a child, their parents must sign for them.

The Big Day

The teachers and the students at the school all talked to Jo about her part in the film. They were very proud of her.

Finally, the big day arrived. Jo was so excited she woke up an hour before the alarm clock rang. It was only 4.30 in the morning. "This is the day I become a film star," she thought.

Jo had to get up very early to get to the film studio on time. At half past six, a car arrived outside Jo's front door. It was Kirsty from the film studio. Her job was to look after Jo when she was at the studio.

Jo had to be at the studio at seven o'clock every day. The people at the studio needed time to make her look like a creature from another planet.

Kirsty and Jo drove to the studio. When Jo saw it for the first time she was amazed at the size of it. "It's huge," she said.

"I know," said Kirsty. "They make a lot of films at the same time, so they need a lot of different studios. Be careful you don't get lost!"

Kirsty and Jo went to the studio where they were filming *Starsearcher*. When they arrived, a man in a uniform checked Jo's name on a list. Then he gave her a security card. She had to show this every time she went into the studio.

Studio
Universal Studios at Orlando, Florida, is the largest studio complex in the world. Did you know that it has its own police department?

Kirsty took Jo through the studio to the make-up department. They entered a room which had a lot of mirrors on the walls. There were a lot of people in the room already. Jo was a little surprised. It was very noisy and busy and it was only 7.15 a.m.

Jo could see some people were sitting in chairs in front of the mirrors. These were the actors. The other people in the room were changing the actors into creatures from Spartalus!

Kirsty pointed to an empty chair and Jo sat in it. She felt a little tense. The lights above the mirror were very bright and hot.

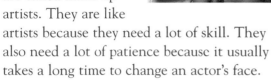

Make-up
The people who change the appearance of actors are called make-up artists. They are like artists because they need a lot of skill. They also need a lot of patience because it usually takes a long time to change an actor's face.

Jo was happy when she saw her make-up artist. He was a handsome young man with a big smile on his face. His name was Scott. He looked like a film star.

"Just relax, young lady," said Scott. "I'm going to make you into a space creature. You won't recognize yourself in two hours."

Jo watched what he was doing in the mirror. First, Scott put a plastic mask over her head and hair. There was some glue on the inside of the mask and it felt very cold. "The glue helps the mask to stay on your head," said Scott. "I know the mask feels strange, but in a few days you will forget that you are wearing it." Jo looked in the mirror. The mask made Jo look funny and she laughed at herself.

Scott started to paint the mask and he asked Jo to keep very still. He put a lot of different colours on the mask. Then he painted spots and lines on it. Finally, he painted blue lines all over the top of Jo's head. "You have no hair," Scott said, "and people can see your veins through your skin."

Jo closed her eyes after a while and relaxed. When she looked in the mirror about two hours later, she got a shock and she nearly jumped out of the chair. She was now an alien! Jo was now Zanuck. She looked exactly like the picture of Zanuck in the storyboard.

Kirsty came into the room and laughed when she saw Jo.

"Okay, Zanuck! It's time to get out of your chair," she shouted. "We have another appointment."

"Where are we going?" Jo asked.

"We're going to the wardrobe department to get you some new clothes!"

Jo was excited and whispered, "Do you think we might see Deborah Ray there?"

"No chance," laughed Kirsty.

"But why not? They also need clothes, don't they?"

"Yes, they do. But the big stars get a personal dresser to look after them."

Costume designers
The people who design the clothes for actors are called costume designers. They need a lot of skill and knowledge.

When they arrived at the wardrobe department, one of the assistants took them to a big room. There were thousands of different kinds of clothes and costumes in the room. Jo recognized some of the clothes from different periods in history. What a wonderful place!

Buzz, the assistant, took Jo to a section where there were some very strange costumes. They were shapes she didn't recognize and some of them were very bright and colourful.

"Here we are," said Buzz, as he took out a light brown costume. Jo thought it looked like the skin of a crocodile. When she touched it, she noticed that it had scales on it. "Just like the skin of a snake or a fish," she thought.

"Where do you get all these amazing costumes?"

"The costume designers draw the costumes and we have lots of tailors who make them," said Buzz. "We keep all the costumes here, and it's my job to find a costume that fits you. Try this one."

After a while, they found one that fitted Jo perfectly. Jo stood in front of a mirror and couldn't believe what she now saw. Kirsty came back and looked at Jo and laughed again. "Not even your parents will recognize you!"

"When do I start acting?" Jo asked.

"In about half an hour," Kirsty said.

"Where do we make the film?"

"We have to go to another part of the studio," said Kirsty. "We have to go to the set for *Starsearcher*."

"What's a set?"

"Well, you are a creature from another planet, so the people in the studio have to build that planet. Not the whole planet, of course! Only parts of it. Let's go and look at your set."

Kirsty and Jo walked to a very large building. They saw a door with the words "Sound Stage B" on it. Kirsty opened it and Jo looked inside. It was very big. It looked about ten times bigger than the school hall. "What a stage!" Jo thought.

There were a lot of people on the set. Carpenters were sawing pieces of wood and making parts for the set. Other people were painting these objects and the walls of the set.

A woman was standing in the middle of the room with a big piece of paper in her hands.

Jo pointed to her and asked, "Who is that?"

"That's the production designer," Kirsty said. "It's her job to design the set. She's looking at the plans for the set and she's checking that everything is in the right place."

Jo walked around the set. It was amazing. There were so many different parts to it. While Jo walked around, she began to feel she really was on another planet. Sometimes, she was inside a building on the planet, then she was on the surface of the planet. It was like a dream.

Suddenly, Jo realized she was lost. She didn't know how to get back to the entrance of the set. Then she remembered something from the film script.

In the film, Zara has to find a magic crystal. She needs this crystal to save the planet. To get the crystal, she must find her way through a maze. "I'm just like Zara," thought Jo. "I'll find my way to the entrance of the set by myself."

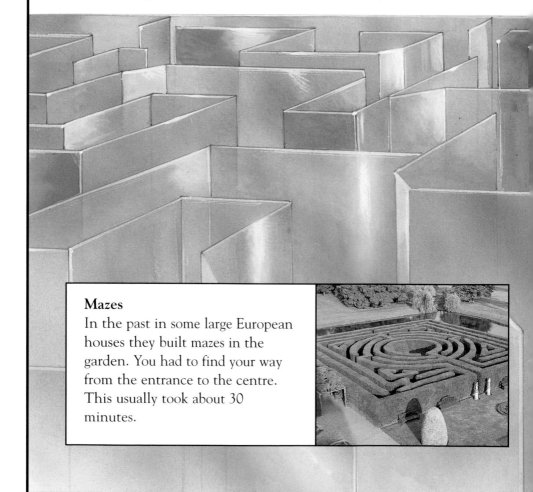

Mazes
In the past in some large European houses they built mazes in the garden. You had to find your way from the entrance to the centre. This usually took about 30 minutes.

The set was just like a maze. There were many paths. Jo went left, then she went right. She tried many different paths but she didn't see anything she recognized. "Where am I?" Jo thought. She began to feel a little afraid.

Jo started to run. Suddenly she reached a dead end. There was no way to go, no way out. She didn't know what to do so she shouted, "Help! Can anybody hear me? I'm lost."

A few minutes later, a carpenter appeared.

"Don't worry. A lot of people get lost in here," he said. He smiled. "Just follow me."

Five minutes later, Kirsty was very happy to see Jo again.

"Where have you been? I was getting worried."

Lights, Camera, Action!

Kirsty took Jo to another part of the studio. It was time to film or, to use movie language, "to shoot" the first scene.

When they reached the set, Jo couldn't believe her eyes. There were so many people there. She didn't expect this. You never see all these people on films. Kirsty saw the look on Jo's face and said, "These are the people behind the scenes."

There were people who had to work the cameras. There were people with microphones. There were lots of technicians who were moving big lights around the room. "I didn't know they needed so many lights to make a film," Jo thought.

Then she saw some of the make-up artists. There were also a lot of other people Jo didn't recognize. "I didn't know it took so many people to make a film," she thought. Kirsty held Jo's hand and whispered, "You'll be fine."

Jo began to practise her lines in her head. She said her words over and over again.

Kirsty could see that Jo was still a little nervous. "Try to imagine that these people are your friends. It's just like acting at school," she said.

"Thanks," Jo replied. "I'll try."

Then a woman came over to Jo and took her onto the set. She was the assistant director. Everybody called her AD.

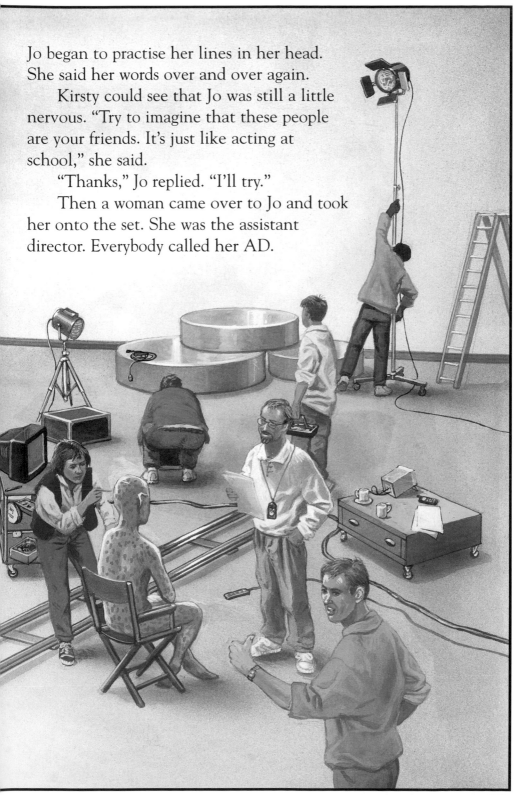

Director
The director is the person who tells the actors what to do. Some directors have more than one job. James Cameron directed the movie *Titanic*. He wrote the script for the film and found the money to make it.

The AD took Jo across the set to meet the director. The director is the most important person on a film set. Somebody has to tell the actors what to do and what to say. This can change many times. This is the director's job. He or she decides how the film will look.

The AD introduced Jo to the director and they shook hands. Jo liked him. He had a nice voice and Jo felt comfortable with him.

The director started to tell Jo what he wanted her to do. "In this scene, Zara is telling people that she must go and get the magic crystal. You, Jo, want to go with her but you know she will say no."

Jo listened very carefully. The director continued, "Now you really, really want to go and I want you to show this in your voice and face. When Zara finishes speaking, I want you to run across to her and go down on your knees in front of her. Then I want you to look into her eyes and say, 'Take me with you, Zara. Please. Please take me with you!'"

The AD took Jo towards a mark on the floor. This showed Jo where to stand when the cameras started to film. All the actors had to be in the right place at the start.

"This is your mark, Jo," the AD said. "Remember it, because we usually have to do the same scene more than once. We repeat it until the director is happy with it."

As Jo was looking at the marks on the floor, somebody shouted, "Watch your backs!" Jo turned round and saw a large camera on wheels. It was like a train. It was moving along a set of metal rails.

Jo jumped out of the way and the camera went past her and stopped just behind her mark on the floor.

"This camera will follow you across the floor when you run to Zara," the AD said. "In the film business, we call this a tracking shot."

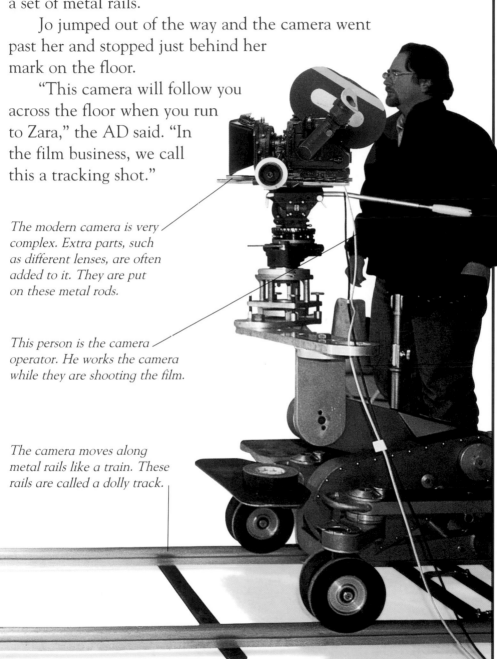

The modern camera is very complex. Extra parts, such as different lenses, are often added to it. They are put on these metal rods.

This person is the camera operator. He works the camera while they are shooting the film.

The camera moves along metal rails like a train. These rails are called a dolly track.

Jo walked over to her mark and stood on it. She was becoming very excited. Once again, she said her words to herself.

While she waited on her mark, a man came over to her with a measuring tape. He was called the focus puller. His job was to measure the distance between Jo and the camera.

The camera needs to get a very clear picture of Jo, so she has to be in focus. After the focus puller measures the distance, he goes to the camera and turns a big ring on the camera. He turns it to the distance between the actor and the camera.

"Right," shouted the focus puller to the camera operator. "She's in focus now."

The camera operator looks through here.

The film is put in the magazine.

This is the lens.

This is the focus ring.

Lighting
When a film is made in a studio, big lamps are used to light up the set. When they are shooting the film outside, the sun is still the best kind of lighting.

Jo continued to wait on her mark. Then another man walked onto the set. He looked very important.

"Who is that?" Jo whispered to the actor who was nearest to her.

"That's the director of photography. He decides which lamps to use, and what kind of lighting is needed. He also decides where the cameras will go."

"Thanks," said Jo. "I hope we start filming soon."

The director of photography lifted his hand high into the air and shouted to one of the technicians, "Flood it."

A few moments later, a soft golden light filled the set. Jo thought it was like the sun rising in the morning. The light made Jo feel a little sad. "Strange," she thought. "This is just how Zanuck has to feel in this scene." Jo was surprised at how the lighting changed her feelings.

After a few minutes, it became very hot on the set. A lot of heat was coming from the big lamps around her. Jo began to sweat. "I hope it doesn't get any hotter," she thought, "I feel like I'm in an oven."

Then a young man came towards Jo with a long pole. Because of the bright lights, she couldn't see him clearly, but he looked like he was fishing. He stopped a few metres from Jo and put the end of the long pole over her head.

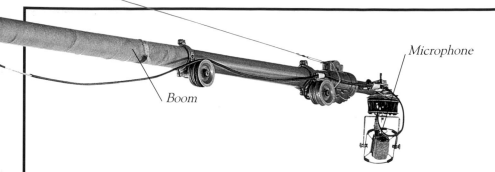

Microphone

Boom

"What are you trying to catch with that?" joked Jo.

"Your voice, I hope!" replied the young man.

Jo looked closely at the pole in his hands. There was a big microphone at the end of the pole, and Jo noticed that he was wearing a large pair of headphones.

"My job is to keep the microphone close to you when we are filming. I have to keep it above you so that nobody will see it in the film."

Just then, Deborah Ray walked onto the set. Jo couldn't believe her eyes. "This is the first time that I have seen her in real life. I've only ever seen her in films," Jo whispered to the young man.

Suddenly Jo's mouth went dry and her heart started beating fast. She felt nervous and she wasn't very sure of herself.

"I don't know if I can speak in front of her."

The director looked over to Jo. He could see that Jo was nervous. He left his chair and came across to her.

"You look very good, Jo," he said in a soft voice. He sounded like her father and Jo relaxed a little. "The casting director told me all about you," he continued. "She said that you acted very well when she saw you at the school. She thinks you'll be a star in the future."

The director went back to his chair and Jo felt more relaxed and confident.

It was time for the first run-through. They had to make sure that everybody knew what to do before they started the cameras.

Jo wasn't happy with the first run-through. She forgot some of her words. Jo was embarrassed and she felt her face get hot.

"I don't usually blush," she thought. "Now I'm glad I'm wearing green make-up!"

There were two more run-throughs and Jo got much better. She remembered her words easily. Then, the director decided that everybody was ready. It was time to shoot the scene.

"Final checks!" shouted the AD.

Immediately, a make-up artist was at Jo's side. She started making small changes to Jo's make-up. Jo felt very important. She felt like a real actor.

The clapperboard
Each small piece of filming is called a "take". There are thousands of takes in a film, and somebody has to put all these pieces of film together in the right order. To help them do this, they use a clapperboard.

The AD walked into the middle of the set with her arms in the air.

"Quiet, everyone!" she shouted.

Everyone stopped talking and looked at the AD.

"Everybody to their marks."

The actors took their positions quickly.

"Run sound!"

The sound recordist checked the microphone and shouted, "Running!"

Next, the AD pointed to the camera behind Jo and ordered, "Run camera!"

"Camera running!" replied the camera operator.

Another person, called the clapper loader, walked quickly over to the camera. He had a clapperboard in his hands and he held it up in front of the lens of the camera. There was some writing in chalk on the clapperboard.

"Slate 66, take one!" he shouted.

The clapper loader moved the top of the board up and down so that it made a loud clapping sound. It sounded like a gun. Then he walked off the set.

Everybody in the room turned to the director. He looked around the set and when he was happy with everything, he shouted, "Action!"

The sound of the clapperboard was very loud and Jo was still thinking about it when the director shouted. She didn't hear what he said. She wasn't paying attention!

When Deborah Ray began to speak her lines, Jo forgot to move at the right time. The director jumped out of his chair and waved his arms.

"Cut!" he shouted.

When Jo heard the director's voice, she woke up and started to move across the room.

"Cut! Cut!" shouted the director again.

Jo kept moving across the stage.

"Jo!" called the director. "Cut means stop!"

"Oh," said Jo. "I'm sorry. I didn't know."

Everybody in the room was looking at Jo. Again she felt embarrassed. She felt her face go red and get hot.

"That's the second time today I've blushed," she thought.

A make-up artist came over and dried her face with a soft towel. She also put a little more make-up on Jo's face.

Nobody was looking at Jo now, so she relaxed and looked around the set.

The lighting technicians were doing something to the lamps. They were putting more coloured sheets of paper over them. These yellow gels made the light on the set very golden.

Gels
Gels are coloured sheets of paper. They are put over the lamps on the set. They change the atmosphere on the set. Different colours create different feelings.

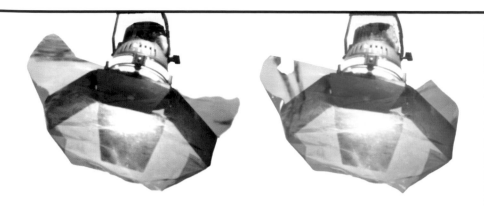

Kirsty came over to Jo and whispered in her ear, "Don't worry, Jo. You looked great and you sounded great. Everybody makes a few mistakes first time."

The AD walked into the middle of the set and shouted, "Okay, everybody. Let's go for another take!" She looked across at Jo and smiled. "Ready, Jo?"

"Yes," said Jo.

The clapper loader called out, "Slate 66, take two!"

This time, everything went all right for Jo. She remembered when to move but Deborah Ray forgot her lines. Jo was very surprised and she felt much better. Even Deborah made mistakes!

"It's good to know that big stars forget their lines as well," she thought to herself.

They tried for a third time, but once again, Deborah forgot her lines. They tried a fourth time, but the director wasn't happy with the way the actors moved.

They had to do the scene six times before they got everything right and the director was happy.

"Come on. Time for lunch," said Kirsty.

Jo looked at the clock on the wall. It was nearly one o'clock. She had breakfast at six o'clock in the morning. That was nearly seven hours ago. She didn't realize how hungry she was.

"I'm starving," Jo said. "Where do we eat?"

Kirsty took Jo to a large canteen in the middle of the studios. It was a very strange experience. There were a lot of actors from many different films there.

"It's like a fancy-dress party," thought Jo.

Jo looked at the strange people sitting at the tables. She recognized the aliens from Spartalus. But there were also soldiers from long ago. They were medieval knights and they wore metal clothes called suits of armour.

There were some monsters from a horror movie. They looked ugly and frightening. Jo decided not to sit beside them.

She went to a table in the corner and sat next to a pirate. He had a wonderful hat with a long green feather in it. He was acting in a film called *Treasure Trove*.

"What do you do in real life?" Jo asked.

"Nothing very exciting," he replied. "I work as a part-time gardener."

Caravans

Sometimes they have to film outside the studio. This is called filming "on location". The actors travel to the location in large caravans. They often have to live in these for weeks.

Jo looked at all the other tables. She was looking for Deborah Ray but she couldn't see her anywhere.

"Where's Deborah Ray?" she asked Kirsty.

"The really big stars have their own rooms or their own caravans," Kirsty said. "Between scenes, they go there to rest and eat."

"That's a pity," replied Jo. "I was hoping to meet Deborah here."

Special Effects

After lunch, Kirsty took Jo back to the set. The director wanted to film a second scene.

"You don't have to worry about this scene, Jo," Kirsty said. "You don't have to say any words."

"What happens in the scene then?" Jo asked. "What do I do if I don't say anything?"

"Well, in this scene, Zara is flying away in her spaceship," said Kirsty. "And you are standing on the surface of the planet. You just look up to the spaceship and wave goodbye to Zara as she flies away."

"That sounds very easy," Jo said. "Let's go."

When they got back to the set, Jo got a shock. There were no buildings on the set. There was just a large blue wall.

Jo turned to Kirsty and asked, "Are we on the right set?"

"What do you mean?"

"Well, where's the planet?" asked Jo. "Or is that blue wall the sky on the planet?"

"No," smiled Kirsty. "This is where the magic starts! That blue wall or blue screen is the background for the scene."

"But what is magical about that?" asked Jo.

"Later, the special effects people will put things onto this background."

"Oh, I see," said Jo. "It's like a film inside a film."

"Yes. The special effects people can put crowds of people in city streets there. If it is a horror movie, they can put lots of horrible monsters and big dark castles there. If it is a war movie, they can put planes and tanks there. These people can put almost anything in the background."

"So will they put Zara's spaceship on the screen in this scene?" asked Jo.

"That's the idea, Jo. You'll see how it works later."

This astronaut is filmed in front of a blue background. The director can put the astronaut anywhere he wants by changing the background.

The director has added a background of volcanoes. He has made it very hot for the astronaut!

This time the director has added a background of streets and buildings.

Filming the second scene was very easy. They only needed two takes to get it right.

It was also a little strange. Jo had to stand in front of the blue screen and imagine that Zara's spaceship was there. This was quite difficult at first.

After they filmed the scene, Kirsty took Jo to a special effects studio where the model makers worked. One man was working with a model of Zara's spaceship. It was much smaller than the real spaceship, but it looked very realistic.

"First we film the model," explained the model maker. "Then we put the film onto the background of the scene that you made this afternoon."

"How do you do that?" asked Jo.

"We have to use computers to combine the two films."

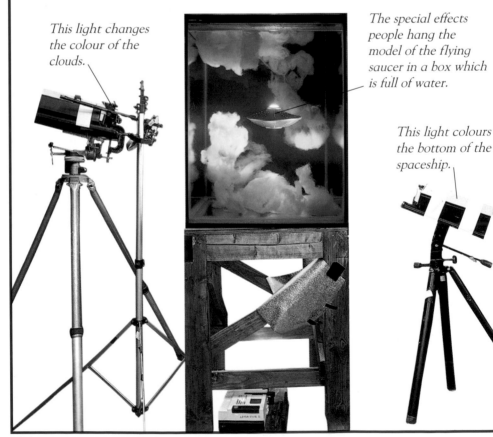

This light changes the colour of the clouds.

The special effects people hang the model of the flying saucer in a box which is full of water.

This light colours the bottom of the spaceship.

The special effects people also use different gels. The gels are used to create different lighting effects on the set.

When they film very close to the spaceship, they use a high speed camera. This makes it look more realistic when it moves.

"That's magic. That's fantastic," said Jo.

"This is a science-fiction film, so you'll have to stand in front of the blue screen," explained the special effects man.

Jo thought for a moment, then she smiled.

"Could you do some movie magic for me?" she asked.

"What kind of magic?"

"In the scene from the film, Zanuck is left on the planet and Zara flies away in her spaceship. Could you do some movie magic so that Zanuck goes with Zara?"

"Sure! We put you in front of the blue screen again, but this time you don't wave to the spaceship," said the special effects man. "This time you hold up your arms. Imagine you have fallen out of a window and you are holding onto the bottom of it. Then we film you in that position."

"And what do you do next?" asked Jo.

"We use the computers to put the two films together."

"Just like you did before," said Jo.

"Yes. We combine the film of you with your arms in the air, and the film of the spaceship," explained the special effects man. "This time we will see you hanging on to the spaceship and flying through space."

In the film, there is a large, green dragon. It stands in front of the magic crystal. The dragon's job is to guard the crystal and to kill anybody who tries to take it.

"Where is the model of the green dragon?" Jo asked the special effects man.

"We need to go to the computer room to see it," he said.

"But why isn't there a model of the dragon in here?"

"Because we don't make a model of the dragon," he said. "Come. Follow me."

The man took Kirsty and Jo to the computer room. A woman was working on a large computer. On the screen, Jo could see a skeleton. It was the skeleton of the dragon.

"So the computer creates the dragon," thought Jo.

"This is called a wire frame," explained the woman at the computer. "We make a three-dimensional picture of the dragon on the computer screen first. Then, we use some software programs to put the dragon's muscles and skin on the picture. That's the clever part. We can make it look very realistic."

"So the dragon only exists in the computer," said Jo. "That's amazing. But how does Zara fight the dragon if it is on a computer screen?"

The programmer can stretch the wire frame of the dragon to make it bigger or smaller.

"We use the computer to move the dragon picture. We can program it to move in many different ways."

"So you make a kind of computer film of the dragon?"

"Yes. That's exactly what we do," explained the woman. "Then we give the film to the special effects people. They combine the computer picture of the dragon with the film of Zara in the maze."

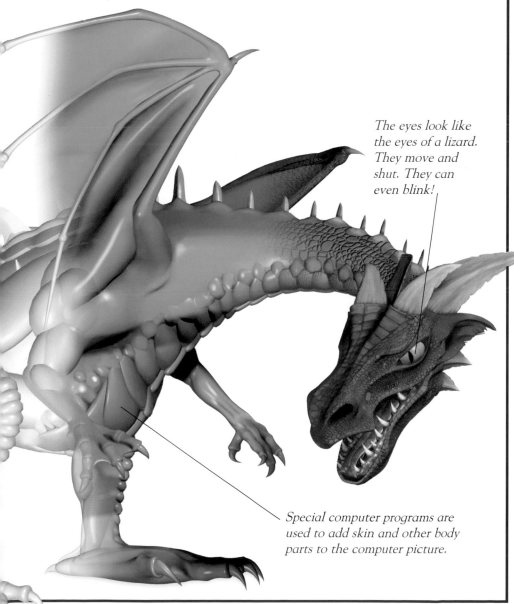

The eyes look like the eyes of a lizard. They move and shut. They can even blink!

Special computer programs are used to add skin and other body parts to the computer picture.

The Final Scene

It was time to shoot the last scene. Jo was very excited. In this scene, Zara returns to the planet with the magic crystal. She has killed the dragon and she can now save the planet.

"After all these weeks and after all the hard work," thought Jo, "I can't believe the film is almost finished."

Suddenly, Jo heard the AD shout, "Where's the crystal? We must find it!"

Props
There are many objects on a film set. These are called props. They can be simple things like pens, or models that cost millions of dollars. These props are from the film *The Borrowers*.

Everybody looked around the room. They had to find the crystal. They couldn't shoot the scene without it.

The props manager looked very worried. His job was to look after all the objects on the set. He had to make sure they were in the right place.

The director looked quite angry. He wanted to finish his film today. "Where has the crystal gone?" he asked the props manager, who started to rush around the set.

Jo decided to go to the toilet while the props manager tried to find the magic crystal. When she went into the toilet, she saw something beside the hand basins. It was shining like a star.

Jo picked up the object and examined it carefully. It was the magic crystal!

Jo carried the crystal back to the set in her hands. She felt like she was carrying treasure.

"Zara!" she shouted. "I have something for you."

Deborah Ray looked at Jo. She was a little confused. These lines weren't in the film script. What was Jo talking about? What did Jo have in her hand?

"What is it?" Deborah asked.

Jo smiled at Deborah and opened her hand. Everyone could see the crystal and they all cheered.

"Well done!" Deborah said. "You've saved Spartalus!"

This made Jo very happy.

Just then, the props manager came back onto the set and Jo told him that the crystal was in the toilet.

"So that's where I left it!" he said. He didn't look worried any more. "Thanks for finding it, Jo. You're a real hero now!"

They were ready now. The AD waved her arms and shouted to everyone on the set.

"Places everyone, and final checks. Let's finish this film!"

Jo stood on her mark and looked behind her for the camera. The camera wasn't there!

"Where is the camera and its little metal rails?" she thought. Just then, she heard the voice of the focus puller.

"Up here, Jo," he said. "Just stand still while I focus the camera on you."

When Jo looked up, she saw the camera above her. It was at the end of a crane. There was a little platform with the camera on it, and the camera operator and the focus puller sat beside it on little chairs. Jo smiled at both of them.

The crane could move up and down. When the director wanted everything on the set in the film, the crane took the camera high into the air. When he wanted a close-up of an object on the set, the crane took the camera down very close to it. The film ends with a close-up of the magic crystal.

On the set, there was a group of Spartalusians. Each one of them had a special gun – a ray gun. A powerful beam of light came out of the gun, and it could destroy things and kill people.

The director told the group what he wanted them to do.

"I want you to run across the set. You are very excited and happy because Zara has brought the magic crystal back. Run towards her with your arms in the air. Ready?"

Everybody nodded and the director shouted, "Action!"

Jo ran across the set. She really did feel excited. She really did feel like she was on Spartalusia. She was swinging her arms and her ray gun around her head just like the director said. But suddenly the gun came out of her hand and flew upwards.

"Ouch!" shouted the focus puller. The gun hit him on the head!

"Good shot!" laughed the camera operator. He lowered the crane and returned the gun to Jo.

They had to shoot the scene again, and Jo held on to the ray gun carefully. There was no accident this time.

Everybody clapped at the end of the final scene. The director looked pleased. He stood up and thanked the actors and all the other people on the set.

Kirsty came over to Jo and put her arms around her. "Well done, Jo. You're a real film star now."

Kirsty looked at Jo with her make-up and costume. She said, "I think it's time to change Zanuck back into Jo. You can't go to school looking like that!"

"I've enjoyed being Zanuck," said Jo.

"I'm not surprised!" laughed Kirsty. "Look at all the adventures you've had. You found the maze, you met the dragon, and it was you that found the magic crystal. Zara is the big star of the film, but I think that Zanuck is the real hero of the film."

Jo felt very pleased and proud. She thought about her friends and asked Kirsty, "When can I see the film at the cinema? I want to see myself on the big screen. I want my parents and friends to see the film."

"In about eight months' time."

"What?" said Jo. "Eight months! Why does it take so long? We've finished the film, haven't we?"

"Well, yes and no," said Kirsty. "Filming is just one part of the process of making a film. There are a number of other things to do."

Jo was learning a lot about films. "What happens next?"

"Well, Jo, the film we shot today goes to a laboratory where it is developed and then printed."

The film is stored on a roll in cans

"I see. It's like taking your holiday pictures to a shop."

"Yes. The printed film is called a rush print, but this is not the final print. First, they send it to the director."

"You mean the director can still change it if he isn't happy with it?" asked Jo.

"Yes, he might decide to film the scene again if he's not happy with it."

"Next they edit the film. Not all the film is used. They cut out parts of some scenes. They might even throw away a complete scene! So don't be upset if some of the things you did are not in the final film! Then, they need to add the voices and music. This is called the sound track. Finally, they add the special effects to the film. There a lot of them in *Starsearcher* so this will take a lot of time. Come on! I'll show you the cutting rooms where they are editing *Starsearcher*."

This is a sound mixer. They use this machine to make many different kinds of sounds for the film, such as footsteps and different voices. They really can make people sound like aliens!

As Kirsty was taking Jo to the cutting rooms, Jo thought, "I've been here for weeks and there are still new places to discover! What a size this place is!"

Kirsty and Jo reached the cutting room where they were editing *Starsearcher*. There was a man inside the room. He was sitting in front of two computer monitors. He was the editor.

Jo shook his hand and asked, "I have a computer at home, but I only have one monitor. Why do you have two monitors?"

"I need them to edit the film," the editor explained. "I need to see two pictures at the same time so that I can put them together."

"I see," said Jo. "What's on the monitors just now?"

"Do you remember the scene early in the film when Zara finds a crystal but then she discovers it isn't the real crystal?"

"Yes, I do!" said Jo.

"On the first monitor, I have the shot of the crystal and, on the second monitor, I have two different shots of Zara's face. Look at them. What do you think she is feeling?"

"In the first one Zara looks serious, and in the second she's unsure of something," said Jo.

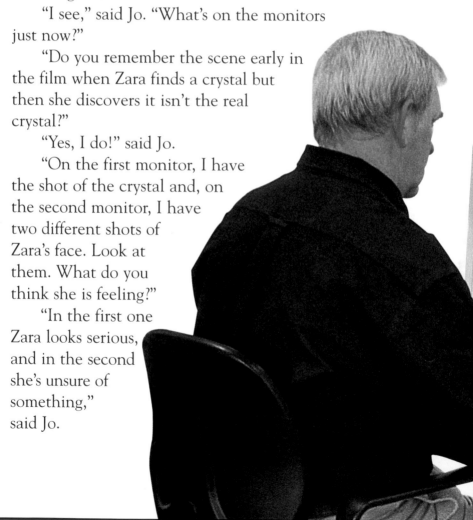

"In the scene, I have to put a shot of Zara's face next to a shot of the crystal," explained the editor. "Now, if I put the serious face next to the shot of the crystal, Zara looks like she doesn't know that it is a false crystal. But, if I put the suspicious face next to it, she looks like she knows there is something wrong."

"Now, Jo! Which picture will I choose?"

Jo looked at the two faces and thought for a moment.

"I think it is important that everyone thinks that Zara is clever, so I think she looks better when she is suspicious of the crystal."

"That's the one I like," smiled the editor.

"Well done, Jo," said Kirsty. "You not only acted in *Starsearcher* but you've also helped to edit the film."

Jo watched as the editor put the two shots together.

"That's what everyone will see in the cinema. Thanks, Jo."

The First Night

Jo went back to school and told her teachers and friends all about the film. Everyone was proud of her. Jo was a real film star.

"When can we see the film?" they all asked.

"It won't be ready for eight months," said Jo.

Everyone was disappointed and, after a few weeks, they all forgot about the film.

Then, eight months later, Jo received a letter from the film studio. She read it quickly. Her eyes opened wide and she shouted to her parents, "It's an invitation to the opening of *Starsearcher* at the Astoria cinema!"

Jo was so excited that she danced across the room waving the letter in the air.

Jo went to the opening night with her parents. She wore a beautiful pink dress and shoes. A large car came to her house and drove them to the cinema.

When they got out of the car, there were a lot of people waiting to see the stars. Most of them were waiting to see Deborah Ray.

There were also a lot of reporters from the newspapers there. They took lots of pictures. The flashbulbs dazzled Jo and, for a few seconds, she couldn't see where she was walking.

Jo felt very important as she walked up the red carpet to the entrance of the cinema. Everyone was looking at her. Some of them wanted her autograph. Jo couldn't believe it. "This isn't real," she thought.

Jo and her parents sat down in the cinema. Then Deborah Ray came in and sat next to them. Jo felt so happy.

As the lights went out and the film started, Jo felt a little nervous. She wasn't sure she wanted to see herself. Then Zanuck, not Jo, appeared on the big screen. Jo was amazed. It was hard to believe that it was really her. "That's me!" she whispered to her mother.

When the film finished, everybody in the cinema stood up and clapped. They all looked towards the stars.

"Are they only looking at Deborah Ray or are they also looking at me?" thought Jo. Then Deborah came towards Jo and lifted her arm into the air. Jo felt so proud and famous! The clapping grew louder.

"I'll never forget this moment as long as I live."

After the film Jo met Kirsty again.

"Well, Jo. How does it feel to be a star?"

"Wonderful, Kirsty. Thanks for all your help but I don't think I want to be an actor when I leave school. I want to work behind the camera. I want to do the special effects. That's more exciting. I want to put the magic into movies!"

Glossary

audition
When an actor goes to a kind of interview to see if he or she is the right person for the part.

assistant director
The person who helps the director to make the film.

camera operator
The person who works the camera during filming.

casting director
The person who chooses the actors who will make the film.

clapperboard
This is a kind of notice that is filmed every time the camera starts. It helps the editor to join all the different pieces of film together.

costume designer
The person who designs the clothes that the actors will wear in the film.

director
The person who makes all the big decisions. This person decides what the film will look like.

director of photography
The person who decides what lights and cameras to use.

editor
The person who puts all the different pieces of film together after the filming is finished.

focus puller
The person who helps the camera operator. This person focuses the camera so that the pictures on the film will be very clear.

production designer
The person who designs the scenes where the filming takes place.

props manager
The person who buys or hires all the objects needed to make the film.

special effects
Using techniques and computers to add extra things to the film, like strange creatures, storms, and travel through space.

storyboard
A simple plan of a scene from the film. It has a number of simple drawings that show what things look like and what the actors will do.

wardrobe
The department that makes or hires the clothes that the actors will wear.